What Is Resurrection?

Basics of the Faith

Sean Michael Lucas, Series Editor

What Is Resurrection?

Joel R. Beeke

P&R PUBLISHING

P.O. BOX 817 • PHILLIPSBURG • NEW JERSEY 08865-0817

ISBN: 978-1-59638-935-9 (pbk)
ISBN: 978-1-59638-936-6 (ePub)
ISBN: 978-1-59638-937-3 (Mobi)

Printed in the United States of America

Library of Congress Control Number: 2014937874

HOW DOES CHRIST'S RESURRECTION SHAPE OUR HOPE?

We all live by hope. If you are an unbeliever, you put all your hope in this life. You get some satisfaction out of life, due to God's common grace, but ultimately your hope is vain, for it will perish. If you are a believer, you build your hope on a different foundation: you build your hope on the sure, unchanging foundation that Christ has been raised from the dead. For you, life is like a long trip or a spiritual pilgrimage to reach Christ and to be with him in glory. Everything about your hope depends on Christ being alive and almighty.

Let us look more closely at how our hope is affected by Christ's resurrection. In the process, we will examine our hope, our life, and our attitude to the resurrection. We will pursue this theme via various portions of 1 Corinthians 15, which is Scripture's most profound, doctrinal defense of the church's confession, "I believe in the resurrection of the dead." Let us specifically focus on verses 19–20: "If in this life only we have hope in Christ, we are of all men most miserable. But now is Christ risen from the dead, and become the firstfruits of them that slept."

A MOMENTARY YET MISERABLE HOPE

The Corinthian Christians did not deny the resurrection of the Lord Jesus, for as Paul says in the opening part of 1 Corinthians 15, hundreds of living witnesses testified (v. 6) of the resurrection. Indeed the resurrection was already part of the apostolic tradition.

Some Christians at Corinth, however, had difficulty believing in a general, physical resurrection of the dead. They could not believe that all believers would be raised like Christ and that their bodies would be reunited with their souls and become like the glorious body of the Lord Jesus.

These Christians were influenced largely by Greek philosophers who believed that, when we die, our souls enter another world but our bodies perish forever. Unlike many philosophers today, they believed that though the body perished, the soul was immortal. Plato, for one, taught that the soul is imprisoned by the body. When someone dies, Plato said, his soul escapes the body like a bird escapes from its cage. For Greek philosophers, the soul was everything; the body, nothing. It was even less than nothing; it was the soul's prison.

Influenced by this Greek philosophy, some Christians at Corinth did not view the bodily resurrection as a privilege. For them, resurrection was purely spiritual.

Today, modern theologians embrace a parallel error. They say Christ's resurrection refers only to the resurrection of the spirit or the teaching of Christ. They claim that the body of Jesus still sleeps in the tomb, but his soul goes marching on. Only Christ's teaching, doctrine, and spirit are still alive, they say. They believe only the doctrine of Christ is immortal. That doctrine, not the person of the resurrected Christ, will one day overcome evil and Satan.

This theology is altogether mistaken in denying the bodily resurrection. It defies the express teaching of the Bible. When Paul instructs the Christians at Corinth about the resurrection, he first strongly asserts that Christ died, was buried, and rose again, all according to the Scriptures (vv. 3–4).

Under the Spirit's enlightening wisdom, Paul then tells the Corinthians the consequences of disbelieving in the bodily resurrection of Christ. In verse 13 he says, "But if there be no resurrection of the dead, then is Christ not risen." The apostle basically says, "If you do not believe in a physical resurrection and deny that the saints will once receive a body like Christ's, then Christ has not been raised, for he is the head of the body, and believers are members of his body. You cannot separate him from his church. If the church will not be raised, then Christ is not raised either. If we believe only in a spiritual resurrection after we die, then we can only believe in a spiritual resurrection of Christ."

The consequence of this denial, Paul says, is the absence of hope and salvation: "And if Christ be not risen, then is our preaching vain, and your faith is also vain. Yea, and we are found false witnesses of God; because we have testified of God that he raised up Christ" (vv. 14–15). If Christ was not raised from the dead, there is no gospel to preach to the lost. There is no gospel of salvation, of deliverance from death, and of eternal life. If Christ was not raised, we have no message of forgiveness, no message of victory over death and hell, no message of eternal life. If Christ was not raised, we have only a momentary hope, which will not carry into eternity.

Christ's resurrection from the dead proves that his sacrifice has been accepted. It proves that his sacrifice has met every requirement of the justice and holiness of God, that God was satisfied by the work of Jesus. If Christ was not raised, the sin question is not settled, the devil is not defeated, atonement is not made, and there is no salvation for lost sinners. If the Lord Jesus had remained in the grave, there would be no Christian faith at all, and His disciples would never have written the New Testament.

If Christ was not raised, our preaching is nothing but a lie, and your faith is in vain. All your trust and reliance upon Christ is an empty hoax. You trust nothing more than a bruised reed. You will be deceived in the end.

We recently witnessed the space shuttle docking with the space station. After they docked, everything in the space station could come into the shuttle, and all the supplies from the shuttle could come into the space station. A remarkable union brought the two together in the darkness. This was Paul's idea of faith: it docked the sinner with Christ. In the midst of the darkness and hopelessness of sin, we look to Christ and dock with him by faith. As a result, all that is in us is transferred to him, and all his righteousness and good works come through the channel of faith and are credited to us.

The space shuttle brought new batteries and sources of energy to the space station, which had lost much of its power. Likewise, when Christ and the sinner come together, the power of Christ gives the sinner power over sin. It enables us to fight against sin and brings power into the heart. What a blessed docking this is between a hell-worthy sinner and the living Christ! As soon as that connection is made, life purges the sinner's bad record and gives power to the sin-fatigued heart.

Paul says here, in effect, that if Christ was not raised, we have no one to dock into. We have no hope of union. We become like any pagan in the street, trying our best to get to heaven by our own efforts. But we are still sinners in the darkness, wandering further and further into outer darkness, with no hope of union with someone who can save us. What a terrible consequence!

Your only hope, Christian, of having your abhorrent records blotted out and all that Christ did written in its place and credited to you is burned into ashes if Christ was not raised! Your hope of gaining power over your habits that are so self-destructive or of getting power from above is gone! It is dashed into pieces! You are still mired in your sins.

Paul goes on to say in verse 18 that those who have fallen asleep in Christ have also perished, if Christ was not raised. In other words, those who died hoping in Christ were deceived in their hope. They have not entered into the place of eternal bliss.

Paul concludes in our text: "If in this life only we have hope in Christ, we are of all men most miserable" (v. 19). If Christ was not raised from the dead, he can only help us believers while we are alive. He cannot be our Savior in death and our Redeemer after death. We can expect nothing from him after this life if he cannot lead us through the dark valley of the shadow of death into the kingdom of his Father. If that is so, we are of all people most miserable. We believers are the most pitiable and unhappy people in the world, for we have placed all our hope upon the Savior's redemptive work—in vain. We have given up the world with all its pleasures and follies and friendships—in vain. We have exposed ourselves to the hatred, the reproach, and the persecution of the world—all in vain. We have been chastised by God—in vain. We have been harassed and tempted by the devil—in vain; we have fought against the world, sin, and Satan—in vain. We have prayed—in vain.

If Christ was not raised from the dead, all our hope, our religion, and our Christianity is a colossal mistake. It is nothing but a dream. Of all people, we are to be most pitied, for we are going to lose both this world and the world to come. If Christ was not raised from the dead, we have no hope or expectation for a better world. We have no future. Abraham and all other believers have sought in vain for a city that has foundations. Moses and the children of Israel have chosen in vain to suffer affliction with the people of God rather than to enjoy the pleasures of sin for a season. In vain we have counted all things loss except for the excellence of Christ. In vain we have denied ourselves and crucified our flesh. In vain we have been oppressed; in vain we have hoped and believed.

But did you notice Paul's emphasis on the little word *if*? Paul says, "*If* Christ be not risen, then is our preaching vain. . . . And *if* Christ be not raised, your faith is vain; ye are yet in your sins. Then they also which are fallen asleep in Christ are perished. . . . we are of all men most miserable!" (vv. 14, 17–19). The apostle is saying in effect, "But God be thanked and blessed; it is not so!" Verse 20 says, *"But now* is Christ risen from the dead, and become the firstfruits of them that slept."

A MAGNIFICENT YET MODERATE HOPE

The truth of Christ's resurrection changes everything. Instead of having only a miserable, mistaken hope, we may now say that we are the most blessed people on earth, for we have a magnificent hope. *Now* we of all people are most happy and hopeful, for God has accepted the sacrifice of his Son, and there is no condemnation to those who are in him. Our faith is not in vain but is the power of God unto salvation. *Now* preaching is full of power and comfort. *Now* those who have fallen asleep in Jesus, expecting salvation from him, have entered into eternal bliss! *Now* all their sins are forgiven and buried in Jesus' empty grave.

This resurrection hope is like a beautiful, glistening diamond in our hands, which we can view from several different angles to appreciate some of its breathtaking beauty. Let's look at some angles of resurrection hope.

The Resurrection's Magnificent Christ-Centered Hope

Our resurrection hope is built on Christ's resurrection in three important ways.

First, the resurrection of Christ is God's validation of Christianity itself. Without Christ's resurrection, Christianity would have been just another sect, quick to die out. But because Christ's tomb was empty on Resurrection Sunday, believers can triumphantly declare: "Death has lost its sting, sin is subdued, the world is overcome, and Satan is trodden underfoot. Christ, who was delivered for our offenses, was raised again for our justification" (see Rom. 4:25)!

On a tour of Israel, we approached the supposed sep-ulcher of Jesus and read on the door: "He is not here, for he is risen" (Matt. 28:6). Our guide said, "This is the best news you'll hear in all of Israel or the world." He was right! It is no wonder, then, that the New Testament believers greeted each other with "The Lord is risen indeed!" Christ's resurrection was the crowning event of his church—the V-Day. It guaran-tees our salvation as believers. These are the two hinges by which the door of salvation swings open: Christ's death and resurrection.

Have you ever cried out in awe, "Jesus is alive! Every stone is rolled away. Redemption is accomplished. Eternal life is secured. Justice is satisfied. The curse of the law is buried. Debt is can-celled. God's amen on his Son's work has resounded through-out the universe, for Jesus is alive. Christianity is objectively, certifiably real and true!"?

Second, the resurrection of Christ is God's guarantee of our resurrection and our ultimate conformity to Christ. Paul says in 1 Corinthians 15:20–22, "But now is Christ risen from the dead, and become the firstfruits of them that slept. For since by man came death, by man came also the resurrection of the dead. For as in Adam all die, even so in Christ shall all be made alive." He elaborates further in verses 45–49:

> "And so it is written, The first man Adam was made a living soul; the last Adam was made a quickening spirit. Howbeit that was not first which is spiritual, but that which is natural; and afterward that which is spiritual. The first man is of the earth, earthy; the second man is the Lord from heaven. As is the earthy, such are they also that are earthy: and as is the heavenly, such are they also that are heavenly. And as we have borne the image of the earthy, we shall also bear the image of the heavenly."

Paul clearly states that our resurrected bodies as believers will resemble Christ's resurrected body. He underscores that in 1 Corinthians 13:12: "For now we see through a glass, darkly; but then face to face: now I know in part; but then shall I know even as also I am known." The apostle John is even more explicit in 1 John 3:2: "Beloved, now are we the sons of God, and it doth not yet appear what we shall be: but we know that, when he shall appear, we shall be like him; for we shall see him as he is."

The resurrected body of Jesus teaches us much about our resurrection bodies. The risen Jesus appeared in the same body that had been crucified. His wounds were apparent; his new body was very much like what he had prior to death. He was recognizable. Although on some occasions, such as with the disciples on the road to Emmaus, people did not immediately recognize him, some familiar mannerism or expression eventually showed them that he was indeed the Lord. Also, his body could be touched by Thomas or other disciples. He was no disembodied spirit or ghost. He ate food with his disciples after the resurrection on more than one occasion, as recorded in Luke 24 and John 21.

Our ultimate end is to be like Christ; therefore, the Holy Spirit is increasingly conforming us to the image of God's dear Son. Paul says in Romans 8:11, "But if the Spirit of him that raised up Jesus from the dead dwell in you, he that raised up Christ from the dead shall also quicken your mortal bodies by his Spirit that dwelleth in you." The Spirit of Christ is a marvelous guarantee of our ultimate destiny in his work in our lives. But even more marvelous is the truth that our existence will be ultimately like that of the risen Christ. That is what we, as his people, can look forward to.

Third, Christ's resurrection guarantees that we will forever focus on Christ in glory. Revelation 7:15 says Christ will sit on the throne of glory forever in the midst of his people. Forever they will bask in his smile, worship at his feet, feast in his presence, bathe in his glory, and delight in his communion. Though they will enjoy the fellowship of saints and angels, Christ will be their all in all (Col. 3:11).

Consider the Resurrection's Magnificent Conscience Hope

The resurrection of Christ is not just the objective cornerstone of our salvation, it is also the subjective hope of our conscience. The Holy Spirit usually leads sinners to that hope by first convicting them of their sin and making room within them for Christ in his resurrection power. He then shows them their miserable hope in themselves. He makes us feel how poor, miserable, wretched, and naked we are in ourselves. We learn what it means to be without God. We learn what it means to be created for eternity, yet be separated from God and from his favor. We feel what it means to be deprived of God's presence and his love.

At such a time, we say to ourselves, "Is there anyone as miserable as me—without hope, without God, without Christ in the world?" We are convicted by our sin. We feel the curse of the law, the judgment of God, the solemnity of our unreadiness to meet him. We see that we will be miserable as long as we are without Christ, for to be without Christ is to be without holiness, without righteousness, without a Savior, without an advocate, without a Mediator between God and us. To be without Jesus is to be under the curse of the law and under the wrath of God.

Every God-taught soul feels the need of Christ. They feel an unbearable burden on their shoulders, which no one but Christ can take away. Normally, the Holy Spirit leads them to see themselves under the wrath of God and to realize that no one but Christ can save them from the wrath to come. They feel the sentence of death in their soul. They are brought to a crossroads: either Christ must justify them or they must burn in hell forever! They must either have Christ to bring them to God, or they must be shut out of God's presence forever. Like a martyr's last words at the stake, they cry out, "None but Christ!" So, if Christ has not risen from the dead, if the justice of God has not been satisfied, if no Savior lives to save sinners, if no blood cleanses from all sin, we would be of all people the most miserable.

But Christ *has* been raised from the dead! That means that our Savior lives and can save us—even to the uttermost. That means the justice of God has been satisfied and salvation is offered freely to lost and wretched sinners.

Some believe that Paul's words, "Christ has been delivered up for our offenses, and has been raised for our justification," refer to a custom in the Middle East. If you want to buy an article displayed in the marketplace, you can bargain with the merchant before deciding what to pay for the article. You then write out your price and lay that on the article. The merchant can either pick up the price or ignore it. If the merchant picks up the price, the offer is accepted.

Well, dear friends, Jesus Christ was delivered up for our offenses on Good Friday! He paid the full price for our sin and iniquity. And on Easter the Father accepted the price; therefore, the resurrection is the cornerstone of our salvation. Without it, we would not know that God was satisfied; we would not know that our sins were blotted out. God the Father accepted the price of his Son! So now, Paul says, "Who shall lay any thing to the charge of God's elect? It is God that justifieth. Who is he that condemneth? It is Christ that died, yea rather, that is risen again, who is even at the right hand of God, who also maketh intercession for us" (Rom. 8:33–34).

When we understand these things by faith and the Holy Spirit applies them to our heart, we miserable sinners are set free in our consciences and we overflow with magnificent and joyous hope in Christ Jesus, which more than compensates for all our losses in this life!

Consider the Resurrection's Magnificent Corporate Hope

Many of us have heard from childhood the question: What is the chief end of man? We readily answer: Man's chief end is to glorify God and to enjoy him forever. You and I strive to glorify and enjoy God in this life. No doubt we also look forward to how we might glorify and enjoy him after death. But I fear we tend to stop at that point. We identify with Paul in Romans 7:24 when he says, "O wretched man that I am! who shall deliver me from the body of this death?" But we do not go on to consider that we will one day fully glorify and enjoy God in our resurrection body. So what a glorious day it will be when the bodies of the dead are raised in Christ! Paul alludes to this in his great benediction in Ephesians 3:20–21: "Now unto him that is able to do exceeding abundantly above all that we ask or think, according to the power that worketh in us, unto him be glory in the church by Christ Jesus throughout all ages, world without end." We gain a sense of that glory and enjoyment in this life as we experience the Lord's work within us. But what will the consummation be like in the resurrection?

In Ephesians 1:18–21, Paul says to believers that they have been enlightened

> that ye may know what is the hope of his calling, and what the riches of the glory of his inheritance in the saints, and what is the exceeding greatness of his power to us-ward who believe, according to the working of his mighty power, which he wrought in Christ, when he raised him from the dead, and set him at his own right hand in the heavenly places, far above all principality, and power, and might, and dominion, and every name that is named, not only in this world, but also in that which is to come.

In a holy and mysterious way, even our Lord's glory awaits the time when he gathers all his people with him in glory and presents them to his Father, saying, "Here am I, Father, and all those that thou hast given to me." Christ longs for the time when he will have his church, his bride, joined to him in the resurrection.

Dr. David C. Jones, writing in the Fall 1985 issue of *Presbyterion* on Jonathan Edwards's dissertation concerning the end for which God created the world, says, "The corporate implications of glorification are not to be missed." Quoting Edwards, he says, "Thus the church of Christ, toward whom and in whom are the emanations of His glory and the communication of His fullness, is called the fullness of Christ, as though He were not in His complete state without her, like Adam without Eve." Jones then says, "Man's chief end is to glorify God in a body, in a corporate entity, organically united to its Head, and not simply as individuals having no connection with one another. This is so much the case that eschatological glorification, which entails the resurrection of the body, is consistently represented in Scripture as taking place at the same time."[1] Edwards writes:

> The supreme good is the glorification and enjoyment that comes in the union of the risen Christ with His bride, the risen church. And the delight of that union will be like the physical and spiritual delight of the union of husband and wife. It is that towards which all of God's creation is leading. That fulfillment of man's chief end, the full glorifying and enjoying of God, will come when we, as His bride, the church, in our resurrection bodies, will be united with Christ in His resurrection body, and we shall be like Him, and so will we ever be with the Lord.[2]

What a day it will be when our whole being, body and soul, praises the triune God forever with no more sin in our soul, no more sin in our body, and no more temptation to sin! We will forever be what we have always wanted to be from the moment of our new birth—sin-free! We will be so sin-free that our holy, spotless Bridegroom will look at us and say, "I see no spot in my Jacob, and no transgression in my Israel."

Amazing grace! I will finally be a worthy, perfect bride in the presence of my worthy perfect Bridegroom, and enjoy an eternally perfect marriage!

Consider the Resurrection's Corporeal or Physical Hope

Our resurrection bodies will have continuity and identity with our present bodies and yet be substantially different. To explain this, Paul uses the image of a seed that is planted and gives birth to a plant. The seed doesn't actually die, yet exists no longer as a seed but as a life-giving nutrient to the plant. Paul's point is that the seed's identity continues in a different form.

We are already familiar with this transition in life. We look at baby pictures of a friend and see some features in the adult that were already evident in the baby. And though we are told that our entire physical molecular composition changes every seven years, we still look much the same. Still, we wonder what our resurrection bodies will be like. If a baby dies, will she be resurrected as an infant? We do not know the answer, but we do know we will be recognizable. When Moses and Elijah appeared with Jesus on the Mount of Transfiguration, Peter, James, and John immediately knew who they were. Likewise, when we sit down to eat with Abraham, Isaac, and Jacob in heaven, we will not need nametags for identification.

First Corinthians 15 offers the fullest explanation of the differences between our present body and our glorified body. In verse 35, Paul asks, "How are the dead raised up? and with what body do they come?" He answers, "And that which thou sowest, thou sowest not that body that shall be. . . . But God giveth it a body as it hath pleased him. . . . So also is the resurrection of the dead" (vv. 37–38, 42a). Paul goes on to mention five differences between our present body and our glorified body in heaven.

First, he says, in verse 42: "It is sown in corruption; it is raised in incorruption." I am dying as I write this. Your bodies are dying as you read this. Our teeth get cavities, our eyes grow dim, our hearing fails us. There is an inevitable process of deterioration at work in every cell in our bodies, which is remorselessly going on until we die. Paul tells us that in heaven there will be no such deterioration. Our bodies will be imperishable and incorruptible. We will be rejuvenated beyond the reach of sickness and injury and death. Imagine what it will be like to have a body that never knows pain, disease, or weakness!

Second, Paul says in verse 43, "It is sown in dishonour; it is raised in glory." A casket contains the poor, weak, wasted shell of someone who has been ravaged by disease. If you look at that poor, dead flesh, which will decay to dust, do you not agree that it is sown in dishonor? But Paul says, "It is raised in glory." I do not know everything that means, but the verse does assure us that in heaven our bodies will be healthy and radiant. Jesus said, "Then shall the righteous shine forth as the sun in the kingdom of their Father" (Matt. 13:43). Our culture puts a high premium on appearance, but no matter what you look like today, you will be even more beautiful in your resurrection body. You will be strong and glorious and magnificent!

Third, Paul says in verse 43, "It is sown in weakness; it is raised in power." How weak we are! We so often have to put up with our lack of strength, our fatigue, our weariness. We get tired and fall asleep, we are stressed and feel we cannot cope, and our energy drains away because of problems and people.

Do you have some disability that you have coped with all your life? Like the lame and blind people who were healed by Jesus, you will one day experience deliverance from that limitation, not only in the functions that you regard as normal in this life, but also in powers you can scarcely imagine. Think of people with mental impairments who will one day operate faster and more accurately than any computer. Think of a world beyond this world of color that will be so multidimensional and so glorious that we will realize what we see today is but a shadow. "Raised in power" means that our bodies will pulsate with energy and dynamism and power. We will not know weariness. No disability will hinder us. We will carry out all the impulses of our holy wills and our holy desires, engaging in continually blessed, worshipful activity forever and ever!

Fourth, verse 44 says, "It is sown a natural body; it is raised a spiritual body." The word *natural* here means our bodies are subject to the limitations of this age, implying they are weakened and damaged by sin. The natural body is what we have inherited from Adam. It was created good, as only God could make it. But what awaits us in the resurrection is even better—we will have bodies like the resurrected body of Christ.

The word *spiritual* here should have a capital *S*—referring to the Holy Spirit. What Paul means is that we will have physical, material bodies of flesh and blood that are energized and ruled by the Spirit. A spiritual person not only thinks about spiritual things, but he also is indwelt by the Spirit. A spiritual body is not a nonmaterial body, but it also is a body irradiated by the Holy Spirit and perfectly suited to the environment of heaven. Our bodies will be the servants of our spirits in heaven. Our body and spirit together will enable us to serve and worship God.

So *spiritual* here means our bodies will be totally submissive to the Spirit of God. Jesus was totally submissive to the Spirit while he was incarnated, yet he was subject to temptation in his natural body. But in our resurrection bodies, we will enter into the ultimate freedom that Augustine says is not the ability to sin that Adam had, or the ability not to sin that the redeemed now have as compared with the inability not to sin that characterized our unredeemed state, but rather, in our spiritual bodies we will have the greatest freedom of all—the inability to sin.[3] Our resurrection bodies will no longer experience the temptations to which we are now subject.

Finally, in verse 53, Paul says the "mortal must put on immortality." All the wonderful traits of the resurrection body already described will not end in death. Our bodies will be the same in essence, but they will have new qualities designed for immortality.

When Christ raised Lazarus from the dead, Lazarus still had to die again. I have often wondered how he felt about that. He must have been torn; happy to be raised for the glory of Christ, yet longing to be with Christ forever in glory. Paul says those raised by Christ at his second coming will not have such mixed feelings. Christ is "the firstfruits" (vv. 20, 23) and "the firstborn from the dead" (Col. 1:18). Those who follow him will be raised with bodies that are immortal like his, no longer subject to death. You can see why Paul, in Philippians 3:10–11, says he longs to be with Christ in eternity: "That I may know him, and the power of his resurrection, and the fellowship of his sufferings, being made conformable unto his death; if by any means I might attain unto the resurrection of the dead." In the end, the resurrection makes us like Christ.

Consider the Resurrection's Chronological Hope

We are tempted to be carried away by our imagination in matters of eschatology. No doubt Charles Hodge is right in asserting that we will all be surprised by some of the events surrounding the second coming of Christ, just as the most godly believers were at Jesus' first coming. Nonetheless, some things appear to be clear in Scripture.

First, Scripture tells us Christ's second coming will be bathed in glory. As Matthew 16:27 says, "For the Son of man shall come in the glory of his Father." He will come as King of Kings into whose hands the Father has given the final judgment (Matt. 24:30). He will come in the glory of his holy angels, which number thousands times ten thousands (Matt. 24:31; Rev. 5:11). Jonathan Edwards says, "Heaven will be for the time deserted of its inhabitants."[4]

Christ will also come suddenly and unexpectedly. The Lord himself will descend from heaven with a shout, with the voice of the archangel, and with the trumpet of God (1 Thess. 4:15–16a). There will be great upheaval in the earth as every grave is opened. Everyone who has died, whether martyred, eaten by wild animals, drowned in the sea, or cremated, will be brought to life.

"The dead in Christ shall rise first," says 1 Thessalonians 4:16. The Thessalonian Christians were concerned that fellow believers who died would be deprived of some of the glory of the Lord's return. But Paul says the dead in Christ would rise first, including people like Stephen, the first martyr, and James the son of Zebedee, John the Baptist, and all the Old Testament saints back to Jeremiah, David, Joshua, Abraham, and Abel. All of your loved ones who trusted in Christ before they died will be there. And if we die before Christ returns, we too will rise at the first command of the Son of God. What a moment that will be!

In 1 Corinthians 15:52, Paul says, "The trumpet shall sound, and the dead shall be raised incorruptible, and we shall be changed." In the twinkling of an eye, you will lose whatever failings of the natural body you struggle with today and will gain all the glories of your resurrection body.

But the primary joy will be the union of Christ with his bride, the church. Those who have already died and those who remain alive will together meet Christ, their Bridegroom, in the air (1 Thess. 4:17). This is the great moment of triumph when the Lord gathers unto himself his own to be with him forever. The prayer of Jesus in John 17:24 will be fulfilled: "Father, I will that they also, whom thou hast given me, be with me where I am; that they may behold my glory, which thou hast given me: for thou lovedst me before the foundation of the world."

Unbelievers who died, as well as unbelievers who are still alive at the time of Christ's return, are not described in these passages. But John 5:28–29 tells us, "Marvel not at this: for the hour is coming, in the which all that are in the graves shall hear his voice, and shall come forth; they that have done good, unto the resurrection of life; and they that have done evil, unto the resurrection of damnation." If there is a period of time between the resurrection of Christ, the firstfruits, and the resurrection of believers, it is also possible that there may be a period of time—be it only moments—between the resurrection of believers and the time when the last enemy, death, is destroyed.

We know that the resurrection will happen, but it is difficult for us to conceive what it will be like, for nothing like it has ever occurred before. There have been raisings of the dead by Christ, by prophets such as Elisha, and by apostles such as Paul. Those who were raised from the dead were offered a foretaste of what is to come. But as Paul says in 1 Corinthians 2:9, "Eye hath not seen, nor ear heard, neither have entered into the heart of man, the things which God hath prepared for them that love him."

Have you ever counted the days to something wonderful that was about to happen in your life? Maybe it was graduation from college, your wedding, or a long-awaited vacation. Whatever it was so energized and motivated you that you could hardly wait for it to happen. Likewise, even though we cannot know everything that the resurrection of the body will bring, we can focus all our energies on the prospect of the greatest wonder of all: to be like the risen Christ and be with him forever. That is the goal of our existence and the hope that inspires all our efforts in this life.

At the resurrection, the souls of the deceased will enter their bodies, never to be separated again. As for the wicked, "death and hell delivered up the dead which were in them" (Rev. 20:13). All shall appear before the eternal Judge. Then, as death leaves us, the judgment day will find us; time will end when judgment day arrives, and when time is no more, change will be impossible. As Ecclesiastes 11:3 says, "If the tree fall toward the south, or toward the north, in the place where the tree falleth, there it shall be."

Unbelievers will then cry to the mountains, "Fall on us, and hide us from the face of him that sitteth on the throne, and from the wrath of the Lamb" (Rev. 6:16), but believers will joyfully gather at Christ's right hand. Jonathan Edwards writes, "Their joy will as it were give them wings to carry them thither. They will with ecstasies and raptures of delight meet their friend and Savior, come into His presence, and stand at His right hand."[5] Every person will be judged, says Romans 14:10, including the saved and unsaved. Every knee will bow, every tongue will confess. All people will be judged according to the degree of light and privilege they have received.

God will open four books: first, his book of remembrance (Mal. 3:16). If we are not saved on that day, all our sins including our secret sins are printed in heaven's book, and God will read them aloud before the whole world. What we dared not tell others, what we dared to minimize and made light of and even forgot, will be exposed to all.

Second, God will open the book of providence (2 Cor. 5:10). All of God's goodness that should have led us to repentance and all our hardness of heart against such providences will be revealed as this book is read.

Third, God will open the book of Scripture that includes both law and gospel. Romans 2:12 says, "For as many as have sinned without law shall also perish without law: and as many as have sinned in the law shall be judged by the law." Those who have the gospel will be judged by the gospel, for Paul says in Romans 2:16, "God shall judge the secrets of men by Jesus Christ according to my gospel." Condemnation will be in exact proportion to guilt, and guilt in exact proportion to abused light and privileges.

Finally, the book of conscience will be opened (Rom. 2:15). If you are unsaved on the judgment day, this book will be worse than a thousand witnesses, for you will have no answers for a thousand questions (Job 9:3).

Believers need not fear these open books, however, for their names are written in the Lamb's book of life (Rev. 21:27). On judgment day, Ephesians 1:4–6 will be fulfilled: "According as he hath chosen us in him before the foundation of the world, that we should be holy and without blame before him in love: having predestinated us unto the adoption of children by Jesus Christ to himself, according to the good pleasure of his will, to the praise of the glory of his grace, wherein he hath made us accepted in the beloved."

None of these books will condemn believers. As for the book of the law, believers experience that "Christ is the end of the law for righteousness to every one that believeth" (Rom. 10:4). The book of the gospel and of the conscience promise believers, as Romans 8:1 says: "There is therefore now no condemnation to them which are in Christ Jesus."

Christ will judge everything: our thoughts, words, and actions; our motives and intentions; our talents and time. Nothing will be skipped. Christ is plain: "Behold, I come quickly; and my reward is with me, to give every man according as his work shall be" (Rev. 22:12). Christ's judgment will be searching, for he says, "I am he which searcheth the reins and hearts: and I will give unto every one of you according to your works" (Rev. 2:23). He will also ponder our hearts and everything we do (Prov. 5:21; 21:2).

Christ's judgment will be impartial, final, and irreversible. He will take no bribes; there will be no parole, no bail, no intermission. Even now, Christ's judgment is near. James 5:9 says, "The judge standeth before the door." Friend, make sure you are ready for Christ's judgment *today*.

Christ will then execute his judgment. Matthew 25:46 says, "These shall go away into everlasting punishment: but the righteous into life eternal." Those who refused to respond to the winsome invitations of the gospel will be compelled to hear the dreadful voice of Christ. As 2 Corinthians 5:11 says, "Knowing

therefore the terror of the Lord, we persuade men." How dreadful it will be to be cast with Satan into hell, to be always dying
but never dead, to be always consuming yet never consumed!

Unless you are born again, God will say of you on that day:
"Bind him hand and foot, and take him away, and cast him into
outer darkness; there shall be weeping and gnashing of teeth"
(Matt. 22:13). Joseph was cast into a pit (Gen. 37:24), Paul and
Silas into an inner prison (Acts 16:23), but there is no pit or prison
like hell. Jesus, the greater Joseph, the Lion of Judah, will cast
unbelievers into the bottomless pit, where the fiery wrath of God
and a burning conscience will eat at them forever. Nebuchadnez-
zar's burning fiery furnace is like ice compared to God's fury in
hell. The city of hell has no exits, the building of hell has no doors
of escape, the society of hell has no relationships. Hell is radical
loneliness, radical forsakenness of the favor of God and men.

"How shall we escape, if we neglect so great salvation?"
asks Hebrews 2:3. J. C. Ryle says, "The saddest road to hell is
that which runs under the pulpit, past the Bible, and through the
midst of warnings and invitations."[6] Make haste for your life's
sake. Flee the wrath to come. Stop putting your heart into this
world, for what will it profit you if you gain the entire world but
lose your soul? Repent and believe the gospel while it is still the
day of grace and salvation.

Christ will say on the judgment day: "He that is unjust, let
him be unjust still: and he which is filthy, let him be filthy still"
(Rev. 22:11). Hell will house no agnostics, but on the day of judgment it will be too late to believe. *Too late* is written across the
gates of hell. Consider, friends, an endless hell can no more be
removed from the Bible than can an endless heaven.

We all are a heartbeat from eternity. So pray with Jonathan
Edwards, "O God, stamp eternity on my eyes." Stamp it on my
hands, my feet, and especially my soul. Consider that if you have
no vision of eternity, you have no understanding of time. Our

lives are not just a journey to death, for we are either journeying to heaven—the eternal day that knows no sunset—or to hell—the eternal night that knows no sunrise. Which destination are you heading for? Are you truly a follower of Christ Jesus? If you were arrested today for being a Christian, would there be enough evidence to convict you?

For you, dear believers, the judgment day means receiving a never-fading crown. Your Savior-Judge will usher you into the heaven of heavens with other believers as one undivided family. He will present you as his bride without spot or wrinkle to his Father for permanent residence in glory. You will dwell forever with Christ, who will feed you and lead you to living waters. You will drink of the fountains of the triune God, praising him for all eternity in holy, glorious activities, many of which are beyond your deepest imagination (1 Cor. 2:9). All that you have experienced here of God and his gracious salvation will be but a shadow compared to what you will enjoy in heaven with God and the saints and the holy angels.

Consider the Resurrection's Comparative Hope

What kept the apostle Paul going in all of his sufferings was knowing that the good he would have in glory would be so magnificent that it would make the troubles of this world seem miniscule. Those joys and comforts consist in both taking away all the bad and in adding limitless good.

All the troubles that we experience with Satan, the tempting world, our old nature, tears and sorrow, ill health, and ill treatment from others will pass away when we get to heaven. We will never again fear temptation, death, falling, bringing shame on our Savior's name, or departing from the faith.

Heaven, however, is not only the absence of sadness, but is also the presence of glorious happiness. Robert Haldane, who witnessed revival in Geneva when he preached to students, cried out with his dying breaths, "Forever with the Lord!"[7] In heaven, Christ will never be out of your sight, dear believer. He will be in your eyesight, before your face, and within earshot for you to talk to, to worship, to question, to understand the Word of Life, to adore, and to thank him for what he has done for you.

Heaven will be a place of perfect worship of God, perfect service to God, perfect reigning with Christ, perfect fellowship with saints, perfect education about God and his truth, and perfect rest. It will be a place of gracious reward for faithfulness on earth and abundant compensation for suffering on earth. Heaven will be a place of perfect holiness—an eternal Holy of Holies and a sin-free land. As Rowland Hill says, "If an unholy man were to get to heaven, he would feel like a hog in a flower garden."[8] Heaven will be pure and clean. There will be no infirmity there and not one speck of dust. All evil will be walled out; all good walled in.

Finally, heaven will be a world of love. Already, God's grace for believers is an infinite and overflowing fountain of love. Spurgeon puts it this way: "It was as though some little fish, being very thirsty, was troubled about drinking the river dry, and Father Thames said, 'Drink away little fish, my stream is sufficient for thee.' "[9] How much more will this be true in heaven! Oh, magnificent hope, magnificent love! Edwards says that God's love in heaven is "an ocean of love without shore or bottom."[10]

Our magnificent hope of heaven ought to teach us not to live just for this life and this world. In living more for the world to come, the Christian should moderate his hopes for this world. Throughout his writings, Paul says that the true Christian has the best of this world, though his heart is not here. His hope in this world falls far short of his hope for the life to come. It is a moderated and tempered hope that comes out of the "now-not-yet" tension of this present age. Now we are in Christ and live by hope, but we are not yet what we will be in glory.

You might say, "What should my attitude be toward this life if I am focused on the life to come? How can I live out this moderate hope with regard to this world?"

Following the teachings of Paul, Calvin teaches us that though we live in hope in the world today, afflictions and cross bearing are necessary for us to learn contempt for the present life when compared to the blessings of heaven. This life is nothing compared to what is to come. It is like smoke or a shadow. Calvin asks, "If heaven is our homeland, what else is the earth but our place of exile? If departure from the world is entry into life, what else is the world but a sepulcher?" He adds, "No one has made progress in the school of Christ who does not joyfully await the day of death and final resurrection."[11]

Calvin uses an argument of opposites to find a middle way between them when explaining the Christian's relation to this world. On the one hand, cross bearing crucifies us to the world and the world to us. On the other hand, the Christian enjoys this present life, but with due restraint and moderation as he learns to use things in this world for the purposes that God intended them. Like Paul, Calvin enjoyed good literature, good food, and the beauties of nature. But, also like Paul, he rejected all forms of earthly excess. The believer is thus called to Christlike moderation, which includes modesty, prudence, avoidance of display, and contentment with our lot, for the hope of the life to come gives purpose to the enjoyment of our present life. Like Paul, Calvin was affirming that, "Here we have no continuing city, but we seek one to come" (Heb. 13:14). This life is always straining after a better, heavenly life.

How is it possible for a Christian to maintain a proper balance so he enjoys the gifts that God gives in this world while avoiding the snare of overindulgence? Calvin offers three principles gleaned from Paul:

1. Remember that God is the giver of every good and perfect gift. This should restrain our lusts because our gratitude to God for his gifts cannot be expressed by a greedy reception of them.
2. Remember that we are stewards of the world in which God has placed us. Soon we will have to give an account to him of our stewardship.
3. Remember that God has called us to himself and to his service. Because of that calling, we strive to fulfill our tasks in his service, for his glory, and under his watchful, benevolent eye, always aiming for the maturation of the saints and the salvation of the lost.[12]

In summary, what Paul and Calvin teach is that a Christian *should not expect to find all joy in this present life*. This truth is obvious but worth stressing because we believers tend to feel sorry for ourselves about having to live in self-denial. Deep down, we don't truly believe that denying ourselves for Christ will give us joy in Christ. We struggle against the unfairness of seeing unbelievers living at ease and in prosperity in this world while we carry our crosses to the bitter end. It is hard to accept that throughout life we must put base desires behind us while all around us people are freely acting out their ambitions. They don't have many restraints, while we are called to be temperate and self-controlled, refusing to hanker for things that the world enjoys but which would compromise our holiness and obedience to God.

Having said that, we go on to say that the Christian has many blessings, comforts, and joys in this life, and God who is rich in mercy has given us these things to enjoy. He keeps back no good from those that love him, even now. Even so, the Christian must deny himself many things in this life and must expect that he will not get full joy in this life because of certain things that belong to the essence of Christian faith and life.

The art of being a Christian is not expecting too much of this life. We do not expect God to give us everything; rather, he gives us only a modest share of joys and comforts. In this world, God feeds us with a spoon. In the world to come, God will feed us with a ladle.

AN UNMOVABLE YET MOVING HOPE

In 1 Corinthians 15:58 Paul says, "Therefore, my beloved brethren, be ye stedfast, unmoveable, always abounding in the work of the Lord, forasmuch as ye know that your labour is not in vain in the Lord." You may wonder why Paul adds this verse after an entire chapter devoted to the resurrection. Actually Paul applies the entire doctrine of resurrection by teaching us that we are not simply to say, "The Lord is risen indeed! Now let us sit back and wait for God to apply the resurrection power of his Son."

Rather, Paul says that because believers are recipients of this magnificent resurrection hope, they must be steadfast and unmovable. What difference does it make whether our Lord comes today or tomorrow, and in a moment or a twinkling of an eye? If he is coming today, I want to be ready. I want to live in anticipation of what will be mine when Christ comes. Paul says that, in rising from the dead, Christ is the firstfruits of those who sleep. So for those in Christ, who now reigns, rules, and brings all things into subjection to himself, the final enemy to be subjected is death. Believers live in anticipation that this "corruptible must put on incorruption" (cf. 1 Cor. 15:53), and they no longer are in their sins but are justified and being sanctified. So "thy kingdom come, Lord, thy will be done on earth as it is in heaven," is a prayer born of this resurrection hope. If you believe in the resurrection of Christ from the dead, the resurrection hope, then you must stand firm—unmovable and steadfast—for Christ and his gospel.

Second, Paul says we are to be moving and active. We must be motivated by our steadfast resurrection hope to become active in the work of God. We must be willing to die every day for the sake of the gospel, says Paul, who fought with wild beasts in Ephesus. Why would Paul do that if Christ had not risen from the dead? But he *has*, and that puts wind in Paul's sails! It gives us strength and hope-filled expectation! It makes us want to be about the business of the King. We want to aim for our Father's glory, for the edification of the saints, and for the salvation of the lost.

Many people around us today have no sense of direction and no future. Their lives are vacuous; they live as though they were just killing time. We have a message for them: Christ was crucified for sinners and raised for their justification. He will come again at the end of the age, and every believer will share in his resurrection victory in the world that will come when he appears. Believe in him so that you may live in hope today and in the world to come.

NOTES

1. David C. Jones, "The Supreme Good," *Presbyterion* 11, no. 2 (fall 1985): 134.

2. Jonathan Edwards, "True Saints, When Absent from the Body, Are Present with the Lord," in *The Works of Jonathan Edwards*, vol. 25, ed. Wilson H. Kimnach (New Haven, CT: Yale University Press, 2006), 225ff.

3. Augustine, *On Rebuke and Grace*, in *A Select Library of the Nicene and Post-Nicene Fathers of the Christian Church*, ed. Philip Schaff (New York: Christian Literature Co., 1887), vol. 5, ch. 33.

4. Jonathan Edwards, "The Final Judgment," in *The Works of Jonathan Edwards*, ed. Edward Hickman (1834; repr., Edinburgh: Banner of Truth, 1974), 2:194.

5. Ibid., 2:195.

6. J. C. Ryle, *Living or Dead?* (New York: Robert Carter and Brothers, 1852), 66.

7. Alexander Haldane, *Memoirs of the Lives of Robert Haldane of Airthrey, and of His Brother, James Alexander Haldane* (London: Hamilton, Adams, and Co., 1852), 612.

8. Vernon J. Charlesworth, *Rowland Hill: His Life, Anecdotes, and Pulpit Sayings* (London: Hodder and Stoughton, 1876), 224.

9. William Williams, *Personal Reminiscences of Charles Haddon Spurgeon* (London: Religious Tract Society, 1895), 19.

10. *The Works of Jonathan Edwards, A. M.*, Vol. 2, ed. Edward Hickman (London, 1839), 889.

11. John Calvin, *Institutes of the Christian Religion*, ed. John T. McNeill, trans. Ford Lewis Battles (Philadelphia: Westminster Press, 1960), 3.9.5–6.

12. Summarized from ibid., 3.10.1–5.